Whitmer Kidnapping Hoax

A Plot to Kidnap Barry Croft Jr. - Nameless Casualties, Secret Wars

Theresa & Tess Nichols

Scriptures are taken from the Geneva Bible 1560, public domain.

Library of Congress Control Number: 2024907237

ISBNs
978-1-958978-23-8 KDP Paperback
978-1-958978-25-2 KDP eBook
978-1-985978-24-5 IngramSpark Paperback

1st edition 2024

Endorsement

As an Air Force veteran and pastor, my aim has been to serve, pursue and protect truth and God's people at all costs. Theresa and Tess have witnessed firsthand the dark forces and corruption that have captured and saturated the greatest country to ever exist. We are imploding from the inside out, and I'm eternally grateful for their hearts and voices that will not stand down, who will represent Christ in the earth, and pull the curtain back on evil.

Pastor Andrew Serafini
Light Dove Ministries

Contents

Prologue

RED PARTY BALLOONS, DR. Atomic exploding targets, BB's, pennies, a green and purple firework, a tricorned man in a PA Walmart ...A formula for a Weapon of Mass Destruction (WMD)!

This is an account of our friendship turned family with Barry Gordon Croft, Jr., our brother, son, husband, fellow Christian Constitutionalist and eternal soul in the purposes of Almighty God. The three of us make up a cord of three strands designed by Christ Jesus our Lord, brought together through the power of His Spirit and forever united in our common love for God our Father.

It is to the best of our ability that we have strove to state all the facts honestly as we know them to be true. We bring to you a faithful accounting of our letters and phone calls to the best of our abilities. We believe in primary source documentation. We are that primary source. We submit this faithful testimony, our communication with him and allow you to listen in on our dialogue with the best man either of us have ever known.

Names have been abbreviated to protect the guilty.

And they overcame him because of the blood of the Lamb and because of the word of their testimony, and they did not love their life even when faced with death.

Revelation 12:11

Chapter 1

Demonic Tsunami Indeed!

IT WAS IN KENT County, Michigan. Everyone's nerves were shot! It was in the midst of the first trial when the letter got passed around. Fights were breaking out and "the kid" had even stopped joking around. It was that night the letter arrived. As soon as it was read, Barry knew he would read it aloud to everyone. The words lifted up everyone's spirit and, for a few brief moments in time, they were not persecuted men. Two of the men simultaneously said, "That's awesome! Whoever wrote that, tell them that I love them!" This was truly a crazy experience.

The Demonic Tsunami took the form of more than a lying, federalist plot. It would be discovered that this Demonic Tsunami would take the form of an inner circle filled with posers and distorters. Subtle subverters. Barry did not expect such embedded infiltration in his connections, both private and public.

Bureaucratic authoritarianism, a brilliant weapon which is the internal Demonic Tsunami, the federalist plot. It is meant to destroy America from within using greed and thirst for power. This government, like an insatiable monster, inhales and devours taxpayers with a feverish gluttony, never satisfied. The government is addicted to the taxpayer dollar and yet there is no possibility to sustain the costs of its ever increasing agencies.

In a moment of divine light and literary genius, we write about the bureaucratic tsunami minus Barry's Ph.D in trucker lingo.

Bureaucracy Killed the Republic

The State Department regrets to inform you that our beloved Republic died today. Lack of personal responsibility and the needs of security and insurance swept it away!

It didn't give up easily, nor did she go without a fight. But the enemy, much too numerous, crept in like a thief in the night.

Under the guise of oaths, never intending to serve or fulfill, the renegades went to work, unsuspecting citizens' blood they spill!

Never expecting something you trust to betray you from inside, but losing sight of liberty, leaving ego, fame and salary to guide.

History will reflect what many predicted would come true. Her end came from within, her own people ran her through.

The "Land of the Free, Home of the Brave," or "In God We Trust," lies we held until the end, as angels shake their heads in disgust!

Proclaiming freedom and Barry's innocence at a "Trunk or Treat" event at a local church. October 31, 2021.

Chapter 2

A Trucker From Delaware

WHY IN THE WORLD would the government target a trucker from Delaware? What were the FBI really after when they attacked Barry Croft Jr. in a WAWA in New Jersey while he made his delivery? What was the real reason for this dumb, insane story about a Governor in Michigan supposedly targeted by a gentleman from Delaware? Honestly, we didn't know anything about Barry Croft, Jr. when we met him. We knew him from his Facebook name, "Last Croft." We knew him as an extremely intelligent man who wore a Colonial tricorn hat with a massive beard, and we thought he was awesome! He spoke of freedom, the Constitution, Declaration of Independence, the Bill of Rights, and he lived it! He lived his freedom on his face, on his tricorned head, and his arms, and on his hands. He's "A Wheel Man," a masterful trucker. He earned this title by being a professional trucker, traveling across this great country, supplying our shelves with all the things our federal notes can buy.

We were in search of "The River" when we met Barry. In October 2019, we became keenly aware of an impending assault on America and our only place of safety would be "The River." The assault would come from within America. It would be perpetrated by the government, its military, and the agencies that were appointed to undermine its freedom. Here is our story of how we came to know and love the man named Barry Croft Jr., a true Christian Constitutionalist. A man targeted for what he knows firsthand, eyewitness facts about governmental corruption. We will tell you the REAL reason the feds targeted him with this kidnapping, WMD (weapons of mass destruction) hoax and why he is in the Alcatraz of the Rockies, USP Florence ADMAX. What you do with this true account is up to you.

Chapter 3

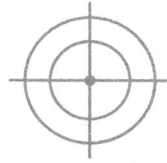

Black Hawk Flyover

YOU NEED TO KNOW something about us the day the military flew over our home in their Black Hawk helicopters. I, Theresa, have been married for 40 years this summer at the writing of this book. My 2 children spent all their years growing up on this beautiful piece of property in the country. My lovely daughter, who co-authored this book with me, stood by my side the day the Black Devils/Hawks flew over our peaceful farmhouse.

On October 7, 2020, we could hear the ominous sound of the propeller blades slicing through the sky over our home, just above our rooftop. These winged black beasts flew side by side directly overhead. This very place where we enjoyed our gardens, our chickens, and goats, sandbox, swings, and pool. We had spent nearly 2 decades splashing in the stream in the backyard, capturing minnows and frogs. We spent hours playing fetch with our dog who was obsessed with chasing the ball. Many nights spent building bonfires and roasting hotdogs and making smores. Every night we enjoyed home cooked meals with our own fresh garden vegetables, bread, and cakes. Thirty-five years of faithful married life with the most beautiful children and home to show for it. Thousands of lovely nights of peaceful sleep when BAM! It was interrupted and invaded by the government's Black Hawk helicopters flying over, low and just clearing the trees, making us aware that they terrorize and target innocent Americans. Instantly we knew that Barry was arrested.

We looked at our phone to call our dear friend. Our Facebook Messenger had been erased with all our lovely back and forth messages about faith and freedom. GONE. The government had moved into our private lives and erased all our proof of Barry's love for Christ and the Constitution. Their criminality was apparent to us. We knew this was an assault on freedom. We knew the narrative they would put forth would be pure dung. Why would the teaching of the Constitution threaten a free Republic? Why would the tricorn be confiscated during his arrest as if "evidence" of an insurrection? And why were his "We the People" and "Expect Us" tattoos considered terrorism? Why would the Alpha and Omega symbols or the III% tattoo on his hands threaten such a mighty standing army as the United States of America? Barry lived his faith. He believes, as we do, that we are created by God with inalienable rights. Rights that cannot be altered, surrendered, transferred or confiscated! Barry is a walking billboard of faith and freedom; the God-given freedom of every single person on the planet. No exceptions! "We the People," is the motto of his life. Just like his motto, he is a man that makes no distinctions. He believes all people are made in the image of God. He is a man who would never be an aggressor. He believes in self-defense only. So how could such an insane narrative be created around such a Christian Constitutionalist with a peaceful posture? Why was Barry accused of plotting a conspiracy to kidnap a Michigan Governor? None of it was believable to us. We know him. We talked to him in text and for hours on the phone. The "almighty" standing army of America would show us the depths of their conspiracy to entrap innocent Americans by flying over our farmhouse. We knew our Christian fellowship with Barry and our love of the Constitution could get us entrapped and targeted, wiretapped and surveilled as well. In the spirit, we walk around with daggers in our backs. The daggers the American government and military plunged into our backs the day they flew over our private property. The day they kidnapped our precious Barry was the day that America showed us her hand. America is an evil empire and dictatorship that won't be stopped until they possess complete power and control over every facet of our lives. The country will fall by its own hand. Barry's life proves that our greatest and worst threat is from within. History will reflect what many predicted would come true. Her end came from within, her own people ran her through.

But still, WHY? Why target Barry Croft Jr. Yes, the Bureaucracy hates Barry's love for and ability to communicate our Constitutional freedom, but enough to hunt him down and label him a terrorist and place him in the worst Gulag in America? What does he know that they want silenced? It's all in the discovery of evidence that was sealed by the Department of Justice. We will tell you what we know. You decide. He's got intelligence on the FBI. He's hiding more under that tricorn than his beautiful bald head!

Chapter 4

They Needed an Excuse

CIA AIRCRAFT SPYING ON Americans on American soil. The Black Hawks proved this to us. It became routine after Barry's arrest that the American government was brutally aggressive in their surveillance. From undercover online employees to fly-overs, drones, contractors, sworn agents on Facebook, threatening phone calls to instill fear or commit fraud, wire-tapping, and blocked 911 calls to report a possible poisoning of our precious Barry while in Terre Haute USP, we had come face-to-face with the beast that had kidnapped and arrested Barry.

The plot to kidnap Gov. Whitmer was flimsy and phony; a made up government plot; a smoke screen for the real reason they wanted him. His friend, KC M. known as KC, was the reason they wanted Barry "taken out." The feds preferred his death, but arrest and buried in a tomb of concrete would suffice. The FBI had 18 CHS's, Confidential Human Sources, attached to Barry going back to 2016. In the discovery, the sealed evidence, Barry saw over 300 FD-1023 forms. These forms are used by special agents to record raw, unverified reports from CHS's, that the FBI generated from mostly people who had never met him. They had a CHS in Delaware on Barry for over a year, and he proved useless because Barry never engaged in criminal activity. This unconstitutional surveillance was employed because Barry knew what the FBI did to KC. They had sent Barry voice clips of them torturing KC. Some of the most hideous sounds imaginable ingrained in the brain of our Barry. Nightmares are still a part of his sleep.

God, his Father, was watching out for Barry. KC's own son accidentally saved Barry's life by telling him that KC's family didn't want him to come to the funeral. Later, though, the feds had the boy "change his mind," but Barry had already situated his work schedule and would not be able to change it. Barry found out that the feds had 4 air marshals planned for the flight he had purchased. They were going to grab him in Texas, and probably would have "suicided" him in his rental car. The Dallas field office has some real killers in it. They did not kill KC themselves. They used CHS's they had embedded in a motorcycle gang called the "Cossacks."

KC was a United States Constitutional Militia man. He backed up the military to defend our southern border. However, before KC ever went to defend the border, he was in that motorcycle gang. When KC quit this gang, he called a bunch of them out for being fed informants. Around the same time this was going down with KC, a girlfriend of one of the Cossacks turned up dead in a bathtub. It was ruled a drug overdose "suicide," except some of her fingernails were torn off. They covered for the man who drowned her in the bathtub. The fingernails were ripped out because they had DNA evidence on them.

The FBI needed to raid Barry's residence. They stole 6 cellphones and the thumb drives. They stole the evidence but not all of it. There's still enough to connect the dots! The unsung heroes are the REAL Constitutional Militia. The feds hoped to expose "The Tricorn Division" by taking Barry out next. The feds swung and missed! The US Constitutional Militia, Tricorn Division, is still out there and they are sworn "death before dishonor!" They are waiting and watching. Some of them are inside the government. They still love Barry, their C-One (Constitutional One), who has been forged in the furnace of affliction! He will come home lookin' like the batman suit! He was on their rear ends like stink on dung. Nameless casualties, secret wars.

Chapter 5

The Truth of Barry's Case

THE GOVERNMENT'S RESPONSE TO his appeal brief was due no later than November 21, 2023 and all it would be capable of containing is conjecture. The FBI had a warrant for all his electronic communications from May 2019 to October 2020, and yet the government could not produce one phone call, one text, one email, nor one supposed encrypted chat between him and his so-called co-conspirators. Not a single one.

Perjury was knee deep with Special Agent H.I. He testified that Barry arranged the Dublin, Ohio meeting and reserved rooms in the Drury Inn. Barry's defense investigative team discovered that all the rooms must be reserved a week and a half in advance. First, in order to reserve rooms, a credit card must be placed on file. Barry's phone call logs did not contain the number to the Drury Inn in Dublin, Ohio. No one can make a reservation without a call or email. The evidence shows that Barry did neither, nor did his debit card reserve any rooms. Second, the FBI didn't think far enough in advance to secure the conference room. A convicted felon and child sex offender, CHS S.R., one of the paid Confidential Human Sources hired by the FBI to do the honored work of defeating domestic terrorism, went into the Drury Inn to secure the conference room. On this Saturday morning in the Drury parking lot, this pedo did what only a corrupt CHS could do. He secured a conference room at the height of the covid bull-dung. How could this sloppy felon convince the Drury Inn to let him use the conference room and stick 13 or 14 people in such a confined space? No ordinary citizen would have been able to make the Drury Inn's management go for that. Not to mention, Barry didn't know 8 or 9 of the people in this group. Complete strangers. He had never met Brian H., Bill N., Adam F., Amanda K. (who brought a 10 year old child), Frank B., Gator, and two young men from Kentucky that were strangers to Barry. Later he found out that one of them was a "CHS" based on a recording in the discovery. Aside from the fact that 4 CHS's were used out of 13 or 14 people, the FBI knows through the warrants on Barry, that he did not know these people, nor did he have their contact information to invite them to a meeting. An example of the perjury an FBI agent is willing to commit can be seen in the lying testimony of Agent K.L. He testified that Barry set up a FTX (Field Training Exercise) to exist simultaneously with CHS S.R.'s "Family Fun Day." An FTX is a summer time camp experience filled with family fun events, barbeques, fireworks and picnics alongside the military and National Guard who interact with the public. Only during the short summer months did Barry attend these events and bring his children during their school's summer vacation. The FBI and CHS plan was to scramble and get Barry to attend in order to develop their plot. Remember, the whole reason they wanted Barry was because he knew about their criminal and murderous actions against his dear friend, KC.

Yet the only people Barry knew at the FTX were the CHS's J.P., S.R. and a guy named Tom L. who Barry knew off Facebook. And since being introduced in Dublin, he became acquainted with Adam F. and Amanda K. Keep in mind, Barry had no intention to attend the Cambria, Wisconsin FTX because of his work schedule. Agent K.L. got CHS J.P. to drive from Tennessee to Delaware, then from Delaware to Wisconsin in order to get Barry to attend that FTX. How does an agent testify that Barry partially set-up this FTX if he didn't plan to attend? And an even more startling question would be, what kind of justice system assists FBI agents in committing perjury? Surely when Judge R.J. heard that CHS J.P. had to be tasked with getting Barry to the FTX, that would've been the spoiler that Agent K.L. was committing perjury.

The facts of this case must come out. We must all ask these questions. In addition, why didn't Barry's Attorney J.B. get all this out in the trials? How come Judge R.J. let the government get away with so much investigative and prosecutorial misconduct, even to the extent of allowing agents to commit perjury under oath?

If these questions don't occur to you or if you just don't give a darn, your freedom is already lost. Then why the heck did our Barry even care? Because KC was murdered by the hands of the criminal government. Barry is living inside of a concrete box for your freedom in the worst prison/gulag in America, the Alcatraz of the Rockies, the Florence ADMAX in Colorado. He's bearing up under extreme deprivation and solitary confinement while you don't even care? If you keep reading, we're going to assume you do.

For KC & the Men and Women of the Bundy Ranch
In the year 2014, Americans were defending our border;
It wasn't our military, and no general gave the order.
That same year found citizens standing, defending private
land;
Not against Chinese or Russians, but a militarized govern-
ment band.
Both were private people, standing for what was right;
Prosecuted by mercenary tyrants, taken like a thief in the
night.
They have truly given some, and some of them gave all;
"All enemies foreign and domestic," by American hands
they'd fall!
Is honor only recognized, in those who collect a check?
How much does loyalty cost, what virtue will you auction off
next?
Money can't buy you love, but it certainly can get you killed;
Which may not bother your conscience, you the taxpayer
paid the bill.
The Tree of Liberty is being watered, and only with patriot
blood;
You sacrifice the humble, those who serve freely out of love!
Don't worry about outside threats, your slayer exists within;
The weapon is authority, and they have what it takes to win!
Other countries will fight, to constrain what you neglected
to do;
It's not us they hate, but the tyrant found among you.

Chapter 6

Firecracker! Firecracker! Boom, Boom, Boom!

THE WMD (WEAPON OF mass destruction) in Barry's case was a firecracker. This firecracker would have some "deadly" pennies taped to it to hold it down so it wouldn't move. It was a make shift flash bang to use in the breach training exercises that never took place at the FTX. It never got used for its intended purpose. So, instead of letting a good firecracker go to waste, it was set off Sunday night before Barry left for home. Neither did the FBI, the mightiest law enforcement agency of the land, identify which potential "suspect" shouted "Fire in the hole!" Turns out the FBI forensics revealed that the pennies traveled a deadly 2 to 3 feet from the boom site.

The truth about the firecracker and how the pennies got involved is all in the interrogation video. Instead of the truth, the feds chose a small, misleading piece of the recording to distort the facts that Barry clearly spoke. The interrogation video is in the discovery of evidence.

The funniest part of all this is the very wording of the statute (law) regarding firecrackers, i.e. pyrotechnics. The statue states that a pyrotechnic cannot be construed to be a "destructive device," even if modified. The truth is that the measurement, and kind of material used in the construction of pyrotechnics, are not high-explosives and therefore cannot qualify as either a "WMD" or a "destructive device."

So, when someone says, "Fire in the hole!" it doesn't matter who said it, all that matters is that the people involved had fun and nobody burned their fingers!

Chapter 7

Physical and Mental Torture...in America

YEAH, YOU HEARD US right. Physical and mental torture, day and night, in America's prisons. The Bureau of Prisons hires psychopaths that love to smash skulls.

Barry doesn't dare allow the prison to address his tooth pain or his shoulder injury. No way. He may not survive their treatment. It's bad enough that he is given "food" labeled "not for human consumption." He sure won't allow them to perform a medical procedure on him.

They put him in Newaygo and Kent County jails in Michigan during the water crisis. The water was so polluted that it could turn a white t-shirt pink and green! Barry lost teeth in that confinement. In Terre Haute USP, Barry would bear up under severe solitary confinement. Under the eternal buzzing of the fluorescent lights, he was buried alive in concrete with the sounds of men down the range being shanked by jagged pieces of metal. It was in this environment that the BOP was up to some strange, extremely demented behavior. In three and half weeks, the staff moved him onto three different "ranges" and four different cells. This psychological manipulation was meant to keep him off balance and make it hard for him to get settled. Seven months of mail and personal items are a lot to keep moving around, all while chained and shackled. Constantly screaming orders and forcing him to move fast, they caused the most duress and chaos possible. It was at this point he would be poisoned and the bottom fell out.

Now that he was off balance, Barry was served a very suspicious piece of "meatloaf." He suspected foul play after 5 bites and stopped eating it. The extreme sickness lasted for 2 weeks, which included vomiting and diarrhea. He had eaten poisoned meat. The Bureau of Prisons cut off all air-conditioning and it was over 100 degrees at this time. In addition, they had a "power outage" during his intense suffering, all the while they pushed his food through the feeder flap and left him to suffer and die by himself. In this intense darkness and heat, the FBI called out a bomb threat. They executed a mass shakedown on an already highly militarized facility! The whole range of men were screaming their fears that Barry's time was up. They were coming for him. The guards shouted at him to spin around and put his back to the door. They chained him from behind in a squat position and left him suffering for hours while sick unto death from the poisoning. It was at this point that our precious Barry wondered who would claim his body?

When finally this trauma ended, he was unshackled and he crashed into his bunk. This would be his first semi-peaceful sleep in 2 weeks. The guards, knowing this, interrupted his healing slumber and shocked him awake. He had missed his call to his beloved during the power outage, but now he was given the opportunity to call her. He was still delirious from the poisoning and the mental and physical trauma of the shakedown. He was handed the phone. Amazingly, in this mental fog, Barry remembers her phone number. He heard the phone connect and he heard her beautiful voice asking with such love, devotion, and concern, "Gunboat (her beloved's name of affection), are you ok?" She instantly knew her Barry was hurt. He could not express a logical thought. Her brilliant Barry had forgotten how to communicate. He had no words. No love. No recollection. We both endured the painful conversation. Heavenly wisdom saved the day. We stayed on the 15 minute phone call and were able to conclude that this was NOT Barry. Who the heck was it then? God's Spirit began to lead our thoughts. Was he drugged? Poisoned? Was it a Bot? An impersonator? Who were we talking to or what had been done to our Barry to make him incoherent?

After that, Barry returned to his cell and his head began to clear as he took his first shower in weeks. He thought he'd been decommissioned for months. So Barry went to work rereading his most recent letters from us. He realized that we were waiting for his first REAL phone call to us and that he, likewise, was counting down the days.

Dandelions are the most over-looked flowers. Just because it is called a weed, does it make it any less beautiful? Dandelions have healing qualities. Together we will bring healing to our Barry

Chapter 8

The Torture Continues

As Barry was coming out of this psychological and physical torment, he wanted to get back to his routine. He would not be permitted to do this. The guards broke into his cell and took all his belongings. Hundreds of stamps he had earned were confiscated. They stole his soap, shampoo, all his blankets, and towels. They took his 3" rubber pens that he used to write to us. All of his property was handled roughly and broken open. It was at this time, he was snatched up and "dieseled" at 1:00AM to USP Florence ADMAX. No warning. No procedure. No protocols. No process and appeals. Nothing. Just lawful criminality. Barry was kidnapped again in the middle of the night.

Having made it to the "Big Suck," he would be deprived of everything their handbook says he is entitled to: paper, envelopes, rubber pen, stamps, clothes, shoes, toiletries. None of it was available. He wasn't permitted to call us for weeks. All he wanted to do was tell us where they transferred him. We found out from a note that he wrote to us on the back of an emergency contact form in the event of his death.

His hunger intensified at the Florence ADMAX. They have mastered the art of starvation. They give Barry just enough "food" to eat in order to stay alive. Every act of the Bureau of Prisons is for supreme control and degradation of an inmate. He has known deep personal humiliation, nakedness during range shakedowns, "Hannibal Lector" like treatment, dog cages, deprivation of communication via phone and mail. The human need for communication is so extreme that Barry discovered that the toilet can act as a means of telecommunication. Here is an ode to Terre Haute, the SHU (Special Housing Unit), death row inmates. P.O. Box 33, we got your number.

Advisory: This poem contains unfiltered, raw language of true events. Terms are cultural and geographic in nature, they are not based on color, but lifestyle and community.

Homo Thugs and Black Mold

Homo thugs, and black mold.
This fagot shit is getting old!
Junkies are fishin' to get that fix.
Smurf downstairs done hit 10 licks!
This dingy cell will make you sick.
Like hearing men, discussing suckin' dick.
I did six years in the early 90's.
Of which this experience does not remind me.
Dead serious yo' men call themselves trannies.
And ain't changed shit, they're cold blooded manly!
I need to leave, get the fuck out the SHU!
Surrounded by insanity, go crazy is all you can do.
All that I know is Terre Haute ain't for me.
Half these men are queer, gay as they can be.
Every once in a while, you need to shake loose.
Grab yourself a redhead, and smoke yo' ass some duce!
It's a daily operation, like that movie Groundhog Day.
Except there are no women, and most these niggaz'r gay.

Chapter 9

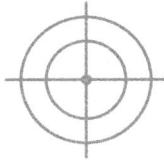

This is Way Bigger Than Michigan

IT OFFICIALLY BEGAN IN May 2019. The Whitmer Kidnapping Hoax originated out of the Baltimore Field Office. With a full investigation that Agent K.L. initiated on Barry based on information received from the Dallas Field Office. This was six months before the FBI employs CHS S.R. and gives him access to a database of Americans that the FBI is seeking to prosecute. After 6 months of a full investigation, which included warrants and full monitoring of all Barry's electronic communications, live surveillance conducted by FBI teams, and all the tools available to the FBI, Barry had committed no crimes.

As of October 2019, when CHS S.R. was hired, no crimes were alleged or committed. Can you imagine the FBI hiring more paid provocateurs when no crimes are being committed? In March 2020, the FBI hired a CHS D.C. Still, no crimes had been committed. CHS D.C. and S.R. have the same story as to why they "came forward." Both have no evidence to corroborate their stories. When the FBI hired CHS J.P. is uncertain. Agent K.L. gave a date in his testimony but it is suspect.

CHS J.P. was hired as an administrator of a "III% National Page" on Facebook. All of the administrators of that page are listed as CHS's in the FD-1023 forms, found in the discovery of evidence. A suspected CHS, A.B., directed Barry to this counterfeit page, where the contact with CHS S.R. and J.P. would originate. However, when A.B. was contacted by a private investigator, DJ N., she would deny knowing Barry. A.B. had been very involved with KC prior to him absconding from probation. She encouraged KC to run, and when he did, she totally disappeared and wouldn't answer her phone. She was also the very first person to call Barry and inform him of KC's death. She had crime scene photos of the body as well. Connecting the dots, A.B. was employed by the FBI to create a web of distortion and entangle Barry, who witnessed the murder of KC.

As you can see, this is way bigger than Michigan. This is a vast network of "CHS"/agent provocateurs, and an FBI database of Americans that the FBI wants to prosecute. It has agent provocateurs embedded in "leadership" roles on social media platforms and an FBI that has positioned itself to create, lead and prosecute alleged crimes at will. The discovery has enough evidence to indict the DOJ and FBI. A FOIA request on the Chase Bank account that supplied the envelopes full of cash will lead to the vast amount of money paid out to the CHS/agent provocateur network. First amendment free speech is gone in America. A Federal Warrant only needs to consist of your Facebook ID number as evidence of a crime. Social media are government made platforms to surveil, target, and prosecute innocent Americans exercising their free speech. And lastly, having evidence and witnessing a crime perpetrated by the federal government and speaking out about it can get you targeted and killed by the FBI. We the People are on dossiers.

Chapter 10

A Criminal Network

THE WHOLE CASE STARTED out by revolving around Barry Croft, Jr. In a criminal enterprise, the highest ranking suspect is called the "ringleader." The government created an unprecedented, new position for Barry by labeling him "spiritual leader." The fact that the FBI and the government would claim that a criminal enterprise is capable of having a spiritual leader is downright crazy. The accusation stemmed from a minute and a half long recording of him telling the story of an actual event in his life. Barry was in his tractor trailer during a riot. He was praying and he asked God if it was okay to defend himself if the need arose. This was the end of a conversation Barry was having with those waiting in the parking lot of the Drury Inn in Dublin, Ohio. While waiting for the conference room the government forgot to reserve in advance, the agents and CHS's didn't turn on their recorders until the end of Barry's conversation! It is this story that Barry tells that this evil government would distort.

Back to the parking lot at the Drury Inn, people were in scattered groups who didn't know each other. Naturally, groups formed as people found others who had some small measure of familiarity. Barry had given a young man from West Virginia, J.K., a ride as he asked him for one. He was in a wheelchair at the time. Barry was getting the chair out of his vehicle as a group formed at the back of his Durango. The narrative of Barry Croft Jr. being the spiritual leader formed there. He had gone next door to the Bob Evans and bought food for everyone to eat. That's where the praying to God conversation started, when he got back from Bob Evans to the Drury Inn parking lot. His passengers, J.K., a devout Christian, and P.K., traveled to Dublin with him, because they saw Barry's post on Facebook. They asked Barry if they could travel with him. The feds know the context of this prayer because they had a warrant to monitor all Barry's electronic communications.

In addition, it is logical that if Barry truly organized any of those meetings, the feds could have used his call logs and warrant captures to prove it. But Judge R.J. kept the CHS cell phone information out of the trial because the government knew its agent provocateurs arranged the whole thing. Judge R.J. was out to cover for the Department of Justice (DOJ). He sealed the discovery so that the American people couldn't see the lengths the FBI went through to create a crime that didn't exist.

Another prime example is a phone call between CHS D.C. and Barry from October 4th, where they talk for an hour and a half, and not one word about the government's fake plan! In that phone call, Barry made it clear that he was going a different way. The DOJ deleted both of Barry's cell phones which destroyed exculpatory evidence.

Just remember, the narrative is constantly changing. The new "ringleader" is now A.F. Just hold on to the real reason for the feds targeting Barry. They have to silence their murder of KC.

Chapter 11

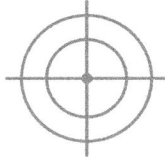

The Feds Are Anonymous Animals

EXACTLY AT THE POINT of writing the chapter, "A Criminal Network," government agents surveilling innocent Americans showed up live on our document. We like to write them messages while they surveil and violate our first amendment rights. This is firsthand, factual proof, that innocent Americans are being targeted for their Constitutional rights. Remember, we are two women from NEPA, who have lived outstanding law-abiding lives of honesty, loyalty, love, and faithfulness. We don't drink, do drugs, smoke, and we don't hang out with people who do. We live holy lives. Absolutely no criminal record. The feds showed up and we have a message for them. They are the demonic tsunami and it is crashing on our free Republic.

Hey animals. We got your number. You are going to go to the abyss, but first, we hope you end up in solitary like you put our

INNOCENT Barry. Why serve Satan, he will only turn on you. You don't scare us. You won't stop the truth from coming out.

These invasions on our computer have happened many times since Barry's arrest in 2020. We have a target on our backs. May the Lord rebuke them.

Comedic Relief! What the feds REALLY look like when spying on innocent Americans. Cue the cool spy music.

Chapter 12

A Promise to Keep

IT BEGINS TO DAWN on Barry that the Bureau of Prisons tried to poison him. The truth that the FBI set up the plot is one thing, but with Barry, he can testify about the stuff the FBI destroyed from the various devices they took from his house and how they murdered KC. There is no statute of limitations on murder, and with it nearly coming up at the first trial, to the FBI, Barry is a "loose end." The FBI is determined to deal with him. The FBI murdered an American citizen in cold blood and Barry had all the evidence on his cell phones, inactive cell phones and SD cards, all of which Attorney J.B. confirmed had been wiped. In a third trial, Barry would most definitely exploit that the government destroyed what is called "potentially exculpatory evidence," which not only warrants a dismissal of the case, but also raises the question of why wipe all of those devices? Remember Barry had only two active cell phones from 5/19 to 10/20. Why would the FBI wipe cell phones that weren't active during their fake plot and why wipe the SD cards if no evidence was found on them concerning the fake Whitmer case? The answer is that those cell phones and SD cards expose a crap ton of FBI paid CHS's and how the

FBI uses CHS's from a motorcycle gang to hold, torture, and murder KC. The evidence is in the discovery and that is why it needs to go public. In it, the feds posed as KC texting Barry, telling him he's starving to death in the wilderness. Telling him he's dying in his Lavoy Finicum t-shirt. Psychological torment. This proves that the feds interrogated him. Posing as KC, the fed mentioned in the text chain a combat ax that KC gave Barry, and tried to get him to admit to "aiding and abetting." They had broken KC and it took them two and a half months to do it. We pray that God exacts justice on them! We hope that God will go "Old Testament" on their sadistic souls!

Even though Barry's devices are wiped, there is still enough evidence to connect the agents from the Dallas Field Office to their two bit cronies in the Baltimore Field Office. It is from that office they brought in Agent K.L. as a conspirator to cover up the murder of KC. The Governor Whitmer plot isn't just a staged fake crime, but a scheme to get Barry in prison so they can kill and silence him. He is the only living witness to the FBI murder of KC. Barry promised KC back in 2018, that he will never leave an American soldier behind. He had no idea what those words would come to mean in his life. KC is gone and Barry is a POW scheduled for demolition in the belly of the Federal/Global Empire/Beast. This is a blockbuster movie, only it's really Barry's life.

"They're not coming for us, are they, sir?" Barry has laid up his treasure in Heaven. Barry asks us if he falls in prison, to see that his name is cleared on this fake fed made hoax. Yes, we will let real Americans know (if there are any left), that right before America fell, it was the citizen soldiers that sacrificed all, while the sell outs and their uniforms helped the Globalists bring down our country. As we walk through the valley of the shadow of death, we shall fear no evil, for God is with us.

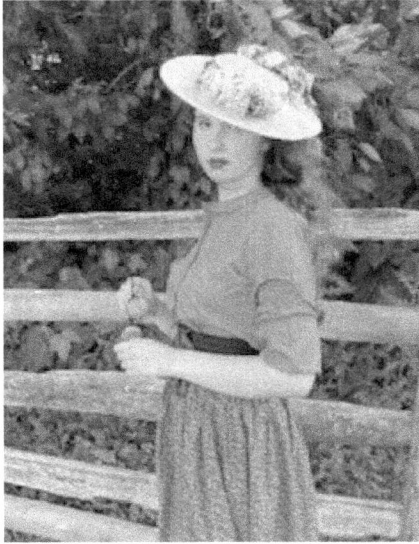

Mom and I met Barry on the battlefield of Gettysburg on July 4, 2020. Now we face a new battle. How do we dismantle a bureaucratic dictatorship?

Chapter 13

Bury the Truth

WARNING: EXPLICIT LANGUAGE TO communicate reality

They make an MF'er not want to piss! Still in USP Terre Haute, Indiana, Barry is exposed to some of the worst conditions and human depravity in America. Fags going at it loudly, a couple dudes just leisurely talking amidst the moaning and Barry just trying to piss! He wonders how in the world did he end up in this cesspool? The most wild, crazy things happen in this penitentiary, all under the watchful, "righteous" eye of the Bureau of Prisons. Men stoned out of their mind with contraband and armed with metal shanks all provided by those who guard and maintain order. Those dudes fished a lawnmower blade down the range! Not a jailhouse shank, but a decapitator! A straight up sword! All of this stuff was brought in from the outside. This is the Bureau of Prisons (BOP).

Barry has the lowest level disciplinary points in the BOP system. According to their own custody classification forms, Barry has never had any write ups or infractions. But get this! He's been placed in a slaughterhouse. They sent him to USP Florence ADMAX (Administrative Maximum). It's the highest level security prison in America! Their placement of Barry into this facility proves further that they are lawless but that's the American government for you. The Somalian pirates who are literal terrorists, who kidnapped a navy officer and stole an emergency escape ship from the Navy, are in the regular population. The BOP has sent Barry to the USP where they put John Gotti, the MS13 gang leader, El Chapo and inmates who murder inmates. The inmates know that the BOP is trying to get Barry killed so that the truth stays buried. All this to show that the Bureau of Prisons prints policy but does not abide by it. They do everything in their power to up Barry's commitment level. Of course, no one will report on the truth. Judge R.J. goes unpunished for violating Barry's Constitutional and due process rights and yet he still has his job to do it to others. And to top it all off, Governor Whitmer was in on the FBI conspiracy. She actually scheduled this crime into her itinerary. Barry never agreed to anything, and the FBI has the surveillance to prove it. Barry was under surveillance since 2017 and a full investigation on him since May 2019. Warrants for all his communication for almost 2 years and they still cannot produce one call, text, message or chat where he agrees to help them with THEIR plot!

The FBI dug into his past, way before their conspiracy was conceived and plotted. They used as "evidence" some patches he designed in 2015, various recordings from before there was an FBI conspiracy, pictures of other guys making an "IED", with no evidence of him conspiring or agreeing. Then the FBI tries to create a crime around his Facebook posts. CHS S.R. asked Barry to put some of his posts on his Facebook page since his account was taken down. The FBI was monitoring Barry and knew all about this. The FBI attempted to create a crime around these posts. Logic dictates that if Barry posted these thoughts from CHS S.R. as his own thoughts, then why wouldn't Barry join their conspiracy when they presented it? Instead, the FBI deleted his cellphones, destroying potential exculpatory evidence. This required immediate dismissal of the case. Attorney J.B. knew they deleted Barry's phones halfway through the first trial. Why didn't he sound the alarm? The voting pattern of the jury was known when the subpoenas were sent out, purposefully pulling from democratic areas with minorities who were brainwashed into thinking the confederate flag meant "We the White People," rather than "We the People." How has the handpicked democratic voters in the jury, with an Antifa jury foreperson, not been reported? And how is "Lady Justice" presented with a blindfold, when law clerks know the voting habits of those they subpoena? As you can see, not only is he buried on the inside of the BOP, but on the outside, the truth is being buried as well. The truth is leaking out though, and We the People must take our heads out of our collective asses.

Chapter 14

Nameless Casualties, Secret Wars

BARRY'S PHONES WOULD PROVE his allegation against CHS S.R. so they had to wipe them, not to mention the evidence of KC's murder and the CHS's the Dallas Field Office used to murder KC. Barry was KC's friend and he knew the FBI killed him. They killed KC because they couldn't use the law to steal his life. He did nothing wrong. He served his country with honor and because he was Constitutional Militia they murdered him. Barry knows the truth. He knows who helped the feds. He knows who looked the other way (law enforcement), other citizens who were victimized, and the motorcycle gang the feds used to commit and stage crimes. How many "suicided" Americans have been killed by fed sellouts? Nameless casualties, secret wars.

Lawless American Justice

Judges who are biased, trials that are not fair;
Justice is becoming extinct, do Americans even care?
Most don't want to accept it, a problem they don't want to face;
Until their lives are in jeopardy, victimized by this disgrace!
A right to face your accuser, in findings of the fact;
Negated by "court rules," in formalities all an act.
They've created fifty shades of grey, in which to mask the truth;
Preventing actual physical evidence, ruled unable to use as proof.
The court can select a jury, from an area that's predisposed;
Before the hearing commences, your position is already opposed.
There's no equality in the law, one side can tamper with a witness;
With the ability to break the law, turning law enforcement into business.
Police can set up a crime, to successfully entrap a citizen;
In a prejudicial system, they are guaranteed to win.
Your lawyer advises silence, so your side no one will hear;
Facing life in prison, a legitimate reason for fear.
They obscure the lack of evidence, the discovery ordered "sealed;"
To prevent the exposure of entrapment and government plot revealed.
Experts at what they do, having successfully stolen my life;
Freedom isn't free, I'm painfully aware of the price.

At rally point and in position. "Spying on the Red Coats and being in love." My Gunboat gave me his Great Coat after I authored the "Research For Further Study" in this book.

Chapter 15

A Willingness to Lie

THE GOVERNMENT HAS PROVEN the lengths they are willing to go to villainize a man they surveilled for 3 years who committed no crimes. It reveals the depth of depravity and rottenness of the FBI, DOJ, CIA, politicians, judges, law enforcement, media, private citizens, CHS's, etc. who are willing to lie. There was no "conspiracy" until mid August 2020, and they knew that, so they lied about June 6, July 11 and July 18 saying "furthering the conspiracy." This is an outright lie.

Further, they accused Barry of being a part of the "Wolverine Watchmen." He had participated in none of their communications. Agent D.C. was second in command of the "Wolverine Watchmen" at that time and Barry was never a part of it and the government knows this. CHS S.R.'s fake militia was called "The United Three Percent Patriot Militia," a fed operative creating a fake militia using "Three Percent" to demonize III%ers, and give the false appearance of Barry's involvement with CHS S.R.'s initiative. He's also recorded in the discovery claiming to be the "National Commanding Officer" of his fake militia of which Barry was not a member.

How does the FBI pay their provocateurs? How do they get all the federal reserve notes to fill their Chase bank envelopes full of cash? The Globalists spent $10,000,000 to frame Barry alone, another $3,500,000 in trials, and they ain't done yet. Why isn't Congress investigating who deposits into that account? How much and who oversees it? Is it another "slush" account funded by illegal drug sales, and other such criminal activity run by the FBI? Where does the FBI get so much cash for nearly 30 plus CHS's that they used against Barry from 2017-2020?

Another huge omission by the government revolved around CHS S.R. who called a surprise meeting in Delaware, early August. They omit this meeting for two reasons. First, the meeting was specifically for sex offender, CHS S.R., to pick up a "ghost" AR-15 from their Virginia target, F.B. Second, at that meeting, F.B. tried to recruit three people to help him blow up his governor's home in Virginia. Barry told CHS S.R. that he never wanted to be around F.B. again. This communication is also conveniently missing from the recordings. Equally important, Attorney J.B. and the defense team failed to bring this up through two trials. Special Agent K.L. was pulling warrants to monitor all Barry's communications for, "conspiracy to injure or impede an officer," from May 2019-October 2020. Based on what? Special Agent K.L. already admitted that this was information received from the Dallas Field Office, but after no evidence of a crime, why were the warrants allowed to continue? And it proves that the judicial branch does not care about rights, but will help the FBI make a case against targeted Americans.

To top it all off, they raided Barry's residence. They found no explosives or illegal firearms. Nothing recovered. Although Barry has been involved in militia work, III%er activities, he has never been involved in criminal activity! The III%er hybrid patch with the Betsy Ross and Confederate flags, were a unit patch copyrighted by Barry for "The Fighting First State Minutemen," a Delaware militia unit, 2014, of which he was the Commanding Officer. The Confederate flag was used only because the Mason-Dixen line runs through Delaware. Once he disbanded it, he didn't mind patriots rocking his unit patch. This true, non-violent militia really made the corrupt government go into high gear. They wanted to erase Barry Croft, Jr. like they did KC.

The Prayer of a Minuteman

My Father, in Heaven, I beg of thee to seek out the heart of thy servant, and preserve it in your grace, that it never be found in the likeness of Cain! May your Spirit, upon which I was made, never be zealous to shed the blood of my brother. In observance of all things dear Lord, evil has always sought to take over what is righteous. Father, in learning to wield the sword of the Spirit, your instructions are always to be of good courage, in faith that you go before us. God in Heaven, whenever you ask whom you shall send, and who will go for Us, please keep my Spirit in mind, not in thirst for blood, but in desire to oppose evil. For when the uncircumcised heart of Goliath, seeks to enslave we who believe in your Son, with their abominations and sin, may we be blameless to go forth as David, to defend your flock. God of Heaven and Earth, let us who pray this prayer please you always, that evil will be forever resisted both in flesh and in spirit, and that our free will reflect your glory, as you are the Lord!

In Jesus' precious Name, Amen!

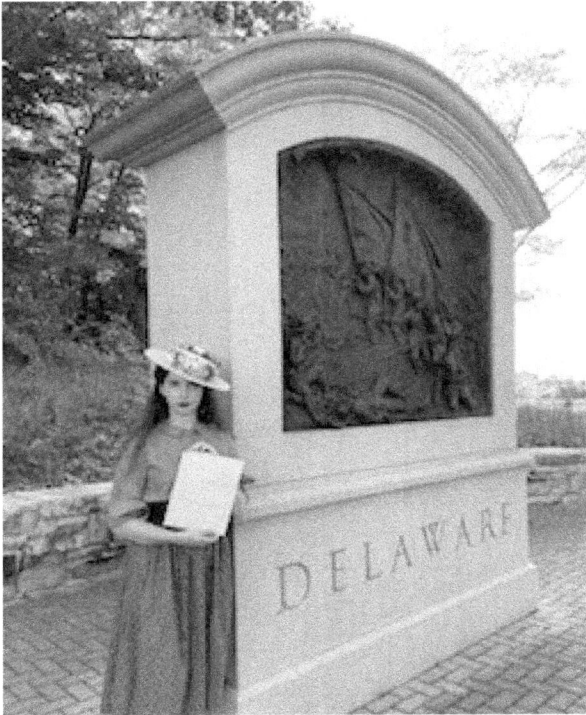

Reading "A Prayer of a Minuteman" in honor of Barry. We specifically went to Gettysburg this day to read that prayer at the Delaware Monument.

Chapter 16

Destination Unknown

THE LENGTHS OF THE government's conspiracy to entrap Americans for crimes that they, the government commits, can be seen clearly on the night of September 12, 2020. Barry was at a Super 8 motel, 45 minutes away from the FTX site. Agent J.C. had a goal for the night and they needed to get Barry in the car even though no one knew exactly what they were doing. Barry was completely unaware of their stupid plot but Agent J.C. and CHS D.C. were planning a drive-by of the Michigan cottage, and coordinated it with Governor Whitmer, the fake victim. They needed to succeed this time so they arranged for 3 cars to participate, all driven by FBI assets or their informants.

CHS D.C. lined up the people to go and set the time for 10PM on 9/12/20. They went way out of their way to get Barry to participate, driving 45 minutes each way. CHS's D.C., T.B. and S.R. were the men in the car that went to pick up Barry from the Super 8. This was so hurriedly arranged, S.R. and T.B. asked D.C. if Barry even knew what was happening.

The three cars met up and were assigned different tasks. Barry would be shuffled into the back seat of CHS D.C.'s car. D.C. drove, CHS T.B. sat next to him. Barry sat in the back with CHS S.R. and A.F. Three paid provocateurs controlling the car and its destiny. The CHS's ask the question, "Where are we going?" Barry answers, "Destination unknown. Destination unknown."

It's in the sealed discovery. Remember all of this is recorded because everyone in the car had recording devices.

The excursion would prove to be a complete fail by the incompetent feds. CHS D.C. would make the stop at the bridge on I-31 as per the FBI's plan. A.F. would take a photo of the bridge that would be used against him at trial. The examination of the bridge would take a minute, all the while Barry never left the car's backseat. That was the excursion of car #1. Total failure.

Cars #2 and #3 had similar failed outings. Car #2 needed to locate the cottage, but, alas, they had the wrong address. So that never happened. Total fail #2. Now it was car #3's try. Their task was to go to the lake and find the boat launch. There, they were to flash their provocateur flashlight to see if CHS D.C. and CHS cronies across the lake could see the light. This part of the excursion succeeded! Mission accomplished! A bright light can be seen in total darkness!

After this failed excursion, the plot had thickened enough to pass it off to a corrupt DOJ who would cover for the criminal FBI.

Barry was returned to the Super 8 where he vomited. He knew he had been among killers. It's these kinds of men who killed KC.

Destination unknown? Not anymore.
Destination known! Our home.

Chapter 17

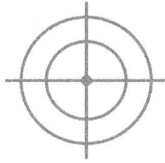

The Bottom Line

THE DISCOVERY OF EVIDENCE proves everything Barry claims. He has been a target for the FBI since 2017 and in 2019 he was upgraded to a HVT (High Value Target). In 2017 KC and Barry decided that there was a need for a real Constitutional militia, no Republicans or Democrats allowed! At the time, Barry was an over the road trucker and a sworn Son of Liberty. They built a network of solid dudes from face to face meeting and association, no keyboard warriors. There were several sections of the United States Constitutional Militia (USCM). There was an interior security and investigative section responsible for keeping the USCM fed free and exposing long time fed plants within the patriot community. Then there was the citizen/soldier section, men who trained and maintained readiness to defend against all enemies, foreign and domestic. By mid 2018, things were going very well. Interior security had identified several long-time plants which included G.H. He would be attached to Barry in 2015 and targeted him for entrapment through his podcast programs which G.H. involved himself in.

It wasn't until 2017 that the reindeer games officially began. G.H. would try to bait Barry into incriminating statements on his program, "Constitutional Restoration Project," which prompted ISI (Inter-Services Intelligence) to do a thorough investigation into G.H.'s history. G.H. participated at Waco. He was implicated in the FBI/CIA's Oklahoma City Bombing. He had too many unpublished details in the feds killing of William "Bill" Cooper. G.H. was an active leader of "Operation Enduring Freedom," which led to the Bundy Ranch standoff. He was also a motivational factor in the Malheur Refuge standoff, and was attached to both KC and Barry Croft Jr. As you could imagine, it created quite a stir. KC, because of his service at the border and having been in fire fights with cartel members, repelling them from entering, KC was the highest ranking officer of the USCM (United States Constitutional Militia.) There were a lot of senior men. Men with prior mercenary (military) experience, men to advise KC in a course of action. But he listened to a young, yankee nobody, Barry Croft Jr. Barry and KC put a vicious counterintelligence operation in place. G.H. and several other bogus plants were fed information on USCM activities. For about a year and a half, they chased their tail! The USCM grew without interference and a special operations group (SOG) was created. Militia special forces was born with the help of an ex-navy seal and a retired two star general. Of course, historically, militia and military don't get along. So what will they call this new unit? It became known as the "Tricorn Division." The feds lost it and decided enough was enough. They put pressure on KC which exacted the effect that they wanted. It was their plan to get KC and Barry at the same time. They were the only two men, at the time, that they knew had involvement in this new USCM. KC obviously didn't break during the torture/interrogation, because they turned their full attention to Barry after KC's death. Barry didn't tell them a thing. The feds know that the USCM is out there somewhere, and the Tricorn Division, but they are clueless as to where it is, because no contact information was allowed to be entered into cell phones. They never recovered the handwritten directory. No one in the Whitmer Kidnapping hoax, or in the discovery, are United States Constitutional Militia. So much for the highest law enforcement of the land! The men are still out there and the feds only got KC and Barry. There are many, many more!

This is the true confession of a real American patriot. There is no statute of limitations for murder! We won't stop until these fed cowards get the needle for what they've done. Not just KC, but Robert "Lavoy" Finicum and the others as well. Remember Croft and KC, two men who faced Goliath to put a smooth stone in their forehead.

The Tyrant that You've Become

It's understandable you don't teach and wish to forget where you're from:

As it must be very uncomfortable acknowledging the tyrant you've become.

Fighting off oppressive rule, our freedom fought for and won;

Now but a distant memory, rejected by the tyrant you've become.

Liberty and justice for all, not selective or just for some;

Contrary to your current status and the tyrant you've become.

Painful all we've sacrificed, hurt so deep it's left us numb;

Our loved ones' lives, forgotten amidst the tyrant you've become.

This land is our home, for us there is no where we can run;

Time to face the beast, and confront the tyrant you've become.

Chapter 18

You are on a Hit List

IT IS IMPERATIVE THAT Americans realize that they are being targeted by their own government. The feds win when there is division, secrecy and silence and they have been winning for far too long! The Stein Dossier is a Department of Justice document that is actually a hit list of innocent, law abiding Americans who are scheduled for demolition. CHS SR was given access to this document that targeted Barry who is now in a concrete box in USP Florence ADMAX. CHS SR is going down this list and targeting his next victim. Remember, CHS SR is a CONVICTED pedophile and felon whom the FBI has employed to take down innocent Americans that the feds wish to destroy. The FBI is a criminal enterprise employing criminals to destroy, imprison and murder innocent Americans that love God and the Constitution.

The database described in the Stein Dossier needs to be exposed! This document lists targeted Americans who are not breaking the law, but the FBI pays agent provocateurs to go out and attempt to ensnare them. This is the same scenario Putin and his FSB does to those he wants eliminated. Again, this database of Americans equates to people who the Department of Justice has essentially put "hits" out on.

We know this to be true. CHS SR had attempted to reach out to us early while pursuing Barry. Since then, an increase of fed operatives have made attempts to attach themselves to us and terrorize us via wiretapping, implanting fake evidence into our phone logs, threatening flyovers, and targeted chemical poisoning sprayed over our home in excess. Police contact websites are blocked and zero follow up when we do contact an officer face to face. So, obviously, the list exists and we seem to be their next target.

The only way to disrupt the feds is to BROADCAST what they will do before they do it! Barry's 6 month review is coming up as this chapter is being written. The step down unit is going to be where the feds make their move. It is where the gang members doing life will be notified of the money on Barry's head OFFERED BY THE FEDS. This happens in low security federal correctional institutions. A young man named KL was stabbed in his hands, back, arm and neck. He was then raped as he was laying there bleeding out. The man who did that to him goes by the nickname, "Monkeyman." Barry was housed with those men in Terre Haute, Special Housing Unit (SHU). Monkeyman had not been charged with the rape and murder of this man while Barry was there. When the feds pulled KL out of his cell, he was still alive. Monkeyman was most likely placed in the same cell with KL because he could have angered the facility with his filing of administrative remedies. It brings vengeance from the staff.

There was another guy from Terre Haute with Barry nick-named "Whitey." This Jewish man was beaten to death. Real life mortal combat matches were set up by the guards. There were men who took "knives" to the recreation cages and con-cealed them in their asses. These Bureau of Prison employees are lawless and quite practiced at covering up their crimes.

Evil lives at ADMAX. It is the Valley of the Shadow of Death. The inmates at ADX are 10 times more dangerous than the mental cases at any other facility. Barry hasn't spoken to a single man there that hasn't killed someone. If Barry defends himself, more charges will be leveled against him. Most of the fights at this level end in fatality.

If you don't want to be their next target, we must broadcast this criminality in the FBI. The Stein Dossier is not a sealed document. It is out there but buried so deep, it is hidden from view. If we find it, you will know about it. We will broadcast it from the rooftops and you can see what this criminal federal government has been up to. Don't participate in their criminal behavior by keeping silent and looking the other way. Sooner or later, it will be your life they seek to destroy. Your number will come up. You are on the list.

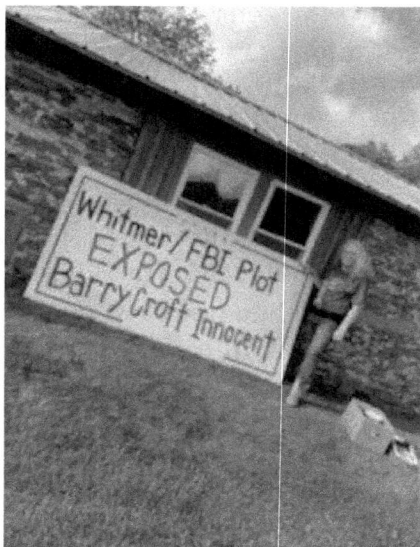

Proclaiming Barry's innocence, the son of my very heart and soul. This sign was placed on the front porch of our home.

Chapter 19

Epilogue

AT THE WRITING OF this book, we wish we could tell you that everything is back to normal. Upon waking up to the bureaucratic tyranny that is in full violent swing in America, normal was only an illusion. Normal never existed and never will.

Our beloved Barry Croft, Jr. is still in the Florence ADMAX in Colorado, enduring the harshest punishment for a government hoax perpetrated by the most sinister criminal empire. America.

If you think you are safe from this kind of surveillance and targeting, think again. You are not. Just reading this book can put you on an FBI hit list of Americans for prosecution. We are eyewitnesses to this very diabolical criminality in the government. Our lives are living proof. Just talking faith and freedom from the privacy of our own home and backyard got us on an FBI hit list. The Blackhawk fly-over is proof of that. Also, the night the BOP poisoned our Barry in Terre Haute USP with their drug-laced "meatloaf," we decided to file a police report 30 minutes after our call with him ended. Our 911 call was quickly answered and we told the dispatcher that we wanted to report a possible poisoning in the Bureau of

Prisons in USP Terre Haute, Indiana. We told them that we believed Barry Croft, Jr. to be in a life threatening situation. We were transferred to speak to "someone else," an FBI agent. We were assured an officer would be right out to take our report. No one showed up at our home. We called 911 again, and the dispatcher sounded alarmed that no officer responded to our first call. She asked if our address was taken. We realized it had not, which proved to us further that they had no intention of coming to our home. She was very helpful and asked us to hold. She returned to the phone line and had changed her tone. She immediately transferred us to speak to "someone else," an agent, that called us by an incorrect name, spoke to us with contempt and tried to create fear. He was unsuccessful. We told the agent that we would not give him any information over the phone. We insisted that he must come to our front door for our report. We told him that we did not trust him. He laughed and mocked our words. We hung up and awaited the arrival of the police. No officer showed up. We called a third time, and our call was blocked! 911 had blocked our number. That night we got a full dose of personal experience with the FBI and corrupt police. Two agencies working together to target Americans. Are we on a hit list? Heck yeah. We oppose their corrupt targeting. They want complete control and domination over us. They will not stop until they have it or God stops them.

We pray that God, who is our Father, will obliterate this Demonic Tsunami that has engulfed this once free Republic. It is a tsunami of global proportions. And do not be unaware, it is demonic. We know what will save this nation. "Find the River!" That is for another book.

LEFT: Our first family photo! RIGHT: A makeover and upgrade!

Chapter 20

Acknowledgments

First we want to thank our God, Jesus Christ, and give Him all the glory, honor, and praise for bestowing upon us knowledge, divine love, and logic. With firm reliance on divine providence, He has guided our minds with countless factual evidence of His love, truth, and His ability to extract justice. We now await, in faith, that He will pay back holy retribution for the evil tormentors that mock the power of righteousness: All in Father's timeline.

I, Tessie Liz, personally need to thank my beloved Gunboat husband, Barry Croft Jr. There aren't enough words or time in life to be able to properly thank him for saving my life. Not only did he define me before Christ, making me his Tessie Liz, but he is also the sole reason for which I was created. I want to thank him for being an American, Heavenly, and Super Hero, God's finest warrior, enduring torture for my God given rights, being my protector, being the best man to ever grace a woman, making me the proudest wife on the planet, and bestowing upon me, the honor of being his woman. I was created for you, my Barry, I'll live for you, I will die for you, and spend all of eternity in every dimension, loving you with my entire existence.

Next, I want to thank my Momma for following the Holy Spirit, no matter where it took her. In obeying the command to find "The River," she delivered me into the arms of my husband, Barry Croft Jr. I want to thank my Momma for raising me to be a God fearing, knowledge seeking, kick ass woman, preparing me for whatever Satan throws at me.

Now it's my turn! I, Theresa, acknowledge the divine leading of the Holy Spirit in my life that led me to Barry Croft Jr. He was God's answer to my prayer. He brought "The River," which I was seeking. His seamless understanding of faith, freedom, and the US Constitution saved my life. Countless hours were spent discussing faith and freedom. He became the son of my very heart, and I am forever in his debt.

I also want to acknowledge my beautiful daughter, my Tessie, who was with me every step of this journey. Through extreme heartache and loss, she proved to be the River of God, stabilizing my soul through the tyranny of a country gone fascist. Her light and love helped bring me to the solid rock, which is Christ. Through Barry's painful incarceration, I have gained a son and a husband for my daughter. Never in my wildest dreams could I have imagined that Father would bring two of the purest "old souls," Barry and Tess, together for one purpose. Together they bring the truth of freedom, proclaimed in our glorious founding documents. These are our God-given inalienable rights.

And finally, we want to thank the Federal Bureau of Investigation and the Bureau of Prisons, along with the countless imposters, posers, accusers, subverters, and distorters, who brought our beloved Barry Croft Jr. into our lives. Your depravity amplified Father's divine love planted in our hearts for Barry. Thank you for the solitary confinement that was used by God to usher Barry into our lives, making us family in this dimension and all dimensions to follow.

Unwittingly, you have served the plans of the living God in our lives. If we never meet you face to face here on this earth, we shall surely see you at the Judgment Seat of Christ, where the angel's discovery of evidence and our own testimony will seal your fate in the eternal judgment of pain and solitude that awaits you in the bowels of Hell.

Chapter 21

Research for Further Study

HELLO, MY NAME IS Tessie Liz. I am a Christian Constitutionalist with knowledge that must be spread throughout America. My personal friend and teacher, now my fiance, Barry Croft Jr., has taught me everything written in this document. Barry Croft Jr., a fellow Christian Constitutionalist, has been falsely accused and imprisoned because of the knowledge he possesses about governmental corruption. This endeavor to shut him up has become futile because thankfully, he passed some of his knowledge on to me. Now I can be a vessel to further the truth by exposing governmental treason.

Hello, my name is Theresa Nichols. I, too, am a Christian Constitutionalist and was granted the privilege of giving birth to Tessie Liz. I am proud of my daughter! Our journey has been side by side in our knowledge about governmental corruption. I was led by God to meet Barry Croft Jr. first. In the course of 4 years, he has become the son of my very heart and soul, and Tessie Liz's husband by vow, fiance by law. This research has been hard earned over years of excruciating, late night and early morning study. It is a part of who I am now. Together, my daughter and I, proclaim the truth by exposing this despotic government. Our Barry is innocent.

It very clearly states in Article 1 Section 1 of the Constitution that "All legislative Powers herein shall be vested in the Congress of the United States, which shall consist of a Senate and House of Representatives. Looking at the bureaucratic dictatorship that we now live in, it is evident that legislative power has been illegally delegated to administrative agencies. The non-delegation doctrine addressed these issues, but are not currently being followed. This leads into the first infraction, the illegal delegation of executive authority to agencies.

It is seen in **Title 3 Section 301 of the United States Code:** "General authorization to delegate functions; publication of delegations." This section of the United States Code illegally gives the President the power to delegate any functions vested in him through the law, and pass it to any agency, without approval or ratification.

To add insult to injury, in **USC Title 5 Section 903,** the President has been given the power to transfer a whole or part of an agency, abolish a whole or part of an agency, consolidate and coordinate a whole or part of an agency, and the authorization to delegate any of his functions. This segues into the President having the ability to create joint agencies, which the **Defense Logistics Agency** has started working on a few years ago. "On February 18, 2021, The Defense Acquisition University spoke with two Defense Logistics Agency leaders to discuss their efforts to unify the interagency with agreements from the Department of Health and Human Services and the Federal Emergency Management Agency, integrating procurement and industrial base expansion, and best practices for succeeding as a joint agency." The act of combining these agencies together will develop a dictatorship; With all powers merged into the executive branch, any chance of justice through checks and balances is vanquished, forming a bureaucratic dictatorship.

It also states in **USC Title 5 Section 559** the words "to diminish the Constitutional rights of any person" has been omitted as surplus usage. Omitting these words demands the general public to only assume that a statute or law will not act in derogation of the Constitution. Obviously, this cannot be assumed. It is extremely evident that we must overturn and abolish this bureaucracy, but those actions have also been prohibited in the USC.

USC Title 10 Section 246, under "Classes of Militia," Constitutional language has been perverted by calling the military, the "organized militia." The Constitutionally proper label for the military, all armed federal agents, is "Standing Army." There is an evident and distinct difference between a paid mercenary and a righteous man willing to leave safety to provide it to those around him. If you scroll down to **USC Title 10 Section 252**, you will see that if the President deems any person a part of a rebellion against the government, he may call into action all or any of the federal agents to suppress the rebellion.

The **military oath of enlistment** has these federal agents swearing to operate under all legal interpretations of the Constitution. They must also realize that "the individual, group, or nation which threatens us could include American citizens..." This leads into the **Department of Homeland Security** releasing their National Terrorism Advisory System, summarizing that all who propagate what they consider, mis, dis, and mal information, and those who undermine the public trust in the U.S. government are to be considered terrorists. What must be done? It is evident that this defacto code is majorly perpetrated by and through lawyers misrepresenting the laws of a Constitutional Republic. I suggest the start of a class action lawsuit against the **American Bar Association**. With the absence of justice, there is no way for We the People to win. We must abolish this junta society, before we are engulfed in tyranny, becoming slaves in the matrix of the bureaucracy.

Each justice, agent, US attorney, etc violates their oath by acting on the USC, but swears to uphold the Constitution. Anyone who takes the oath of office and rules off of the USC will be directly breaking their oath; an offense equivalent to treason.

OATHS OF OFFICE:

- Title 28 Sec 453 Oaths of Justice

- Title 5 Sec 3331 Oaths for Agents

- Title 28 Sec 544 Oaths of US Attorney

UN AGENDA

The UN is a United States created world administrative agency. Below, is a portion that states that any sort of intolerance defined by the world government will be deemed as terrorism. Any sort of belief that contradicts their world agenda will be a punishable crime.

"OP36bis. and requests Welcomes the report of the Secretary-General on, "Terrorist attacks on the basis of xenophobia, racism and other forms of intolerance, or in the name of religion or belief" as an important step in consultation with Member States, to developing a greater understanding of the motivations, objectives, organization and the threat posed by such groups within the global terrorist landscape, including new and emerging threats, and to help to build, upon request, effective counter-narratives, and capacities and strategies in this regard, and to report thereon in advance of its seventy-seventh session;"

To easily find this section of the UN Global agenda, follow these steps. Open up your google search engine and type "UN 2024 Agenda." Click on "Implementation." Scroll down to see "Find a full list of mandates here." Find the dropdown that says "The United Nations Global Counter-Terrorism Strategy: seventh review" Select the "Zero Draft." Under page 13 you will find the portion above. I give these directions in case the link ceases to work.

UN Agenda 2024:

NOAHIDE & UN

"The Institute of Noahide Code is a UN-accredited NGO dedicated to spreading awareness of the Seven Noahide Laws, **which all peoples of the world are obligated to follow.**"

The penalty for violating the Noahide laws is spelled out in the Encyclopedia Judaica on page 1192. "Violation of any one of the seven laws subjects the Noahide to capital punishment by **decapitation**." The UN pledges Allegiance to these laws.

UN Pledging Allegiance to the Noahide Laws: https://www.un.org/ecosoc/sites/www.un.org.ecosoc/files/files/en/2016doc/list-oral-statment-institute-of-noahide-code.pdf

On March 20, 1991 President Bush, Senior, signed into law a Congressional Joint Resolution entitled, "A Joint Resolution To Designate March 26, 1991, As Education Day, USA" In this statute, understand that this is a congressional proclamation of allegiance and obedience to the Noahide laws.

Congressional Statute:

UN International Covenant on Civil and Political Rights "(5) That the United States understands that this Covenant shall be implemented by the Federal Government to the extent that it exercises legislative and judicial jurisdiction over the matters covered therein, and otherwise by the state and local governments; to the extent that state and local governments exercise jurisdiction over such matters, the Federal Government shall take measures appropriate to the Federal system to the end that the competent authorities of the state or local governments may take appropriate measures for the fulfillment of the Covenant." It states under their Declaration, "(3) That the United States declares that the right referred to in article 47 may be exercised only in accordance with international law." Well according to Article 47, "Nothing in the present Covenant shall be interpreted as impairing the inherent right of all peoples to enjoy and utilize fully and freely their natural wealth and resources." This right may only be exercised according to international Law, and those laws are the Noahide laws. National sovereignty cannot be delegated to any other authority, and it most certainly cannot be delegated to international authorities.

1976 DECLARATION OF INTERDEPENDENCE:
This document was made to establish a new world order and to abandon national sovereignty, personal and private rights, and to create a utopia where no one can have an independent thought or belief. This document creates one global authority. This was signed into Congress.

Kamala Harris accidentally spoke New World Order goal, DEPOPULATION:

Regardless of the case the administrative "deep" state brought against Barry and the slander of their lap dogs (mainstream media), we still want to warn our beloved country, and her people, about the methods already in place to take over your freedom. The USC, or the United States Code, has already completely rewritten how your government works! Our Constitution, and our rights, have been taken from us with a process known as "Administrative Promulgation." In Title 3, Section 301 "Delegation of Authority," you will find that administrative department heads are given the same power as our president, "without needing permission, or authorization." This is not something that any branch of the government, (executive, legislative, or judicial), may legally by the Constitution, do! It is done by "Administrative Promulgation." The reason I'm pointing this out is because nearly all of the USC is made up of this promulgation. The "Elections and Voting" title dictates which machines the states may use for voting if they want to receive their budgeted allotment from the government. The judicial branch of government is so unimportant, that the Title 28 "Judicial Procedure," isn't even in the first five titles! Our reason for pointing this out is whether we have Trump who was surrounded by "swamp things/ deep state agents," or creepy, sleepy Joe, the administrative "deep" state running our country! With Trump indicted (bogus case,) and threats of impeaching sleepy Joe, the administrative "deep" state (FBI/CIA) will most assuredly seek to create violent clashes amongst democrats and republican citizens, as they did leading up to the 2020 elections. The violence doesn't even have to be real, they can pay actors with chase banks envelopes full of cash, have the police "stand down," and invite the mainstream media to convince the world that America is at civil war again. This will allow the administrative "deep" state, and all their globalist department heads to invite the UN to "help restore order." Oh yeah, and the recent "railroad accidents" that are placing toxic chemicals in agricultural areas, with almost tactical precision needs to be very thoroughly investigated by someone other than the administrative "deep" state! Please do not brush this information off! Research amongst your brightest colleagues how unconstitutional the USC is, and the "Reorganization Plans" of the executive branch, you will find the "why and how" of our country's current situation. The codification, and creation of the vast all powerful administrative state, is an insurance policy built in by the globalists, to protect investment shortly after the Great Depression of 1929. We beg of you to research what we're saying! Presidents, congress, judges, have all been used to make this illegal process take control of our Constitutional Republic! Please research it! And for the record, Barry Croft Jr. was involved in a plot to kidnap the Michigan governor, as much as Iraq was to ram planes into the World Trade Center. Damn shame what the administrative "deep" state can manipulate the country to believe with their mainstream media! Please,

please, from American Constitutionalists that love their fellow Americans and their freedom, please research these words! Thank you for reading, God bless and long live the Constitutional Republic!

USC Title 3 Section 301-

USC Title 5 Section 903-

Defense Logistics Agency-
https://www.dla.mil/About-DLA/News/News-Article-View/Article/2507187/adaptive-acquisition-unifying-the-interagency/

USC Title 5 Section 559-

USC Title 10 Section 246 and USC Title 10 Section 252-

Department of Homeland Security:

UN Agenda 2024:

UN Pledging Allegiance to the Noahide Laws:
https://www.un.org/ecosoc/sites/www.un.org.ecosoc/files/files/en/2016doc/list-oral-statment-institute-of-noahide-code.pdf

Congressional Statute:

OATHS OF OFFICE

Title 28 Sec 453 Oaths of Justice: PAGE 152

Title 5 Sec 3331 Oaths for Agents: PAGE 305

Title 28 Sec 544 Oaths of US Attorney: PAGE 226

1976 Declaration of Interdependence:

Kamala Harris accidentally spoke New World Order goal, DEPOPULATION:

Air Force Oath of Enlistment: See next page.

THE OATH OF ENLISTMENT

Title 10, US Code; Act of 5 May 1960, with amendment effective 5 October 1962

"I do Solemnly Swear (or Affirm)"

In taking this oath, as witnessed by the enlisting officer, I make a matter of conscience all that is outlined below. When taking the Oath, I create a covenant between myself and that which I hold most sacred. Further, in my relationship with society, I understand this declaration holds me individually responsible for my own actions, words, and promises.

"That I Will Support and Defend the Constitution of the United States"

This Constitution serves as this nation's legal foundation document, and when coupled with amendments and legal interpretations, serve as the basic charter under which our government of law operates, and protects all Americans and our way of life. To preserve this nation, I will uphold and champion its provisions while shielding and protecting it to the utmost of my capabilities.

"Against All Enemies, Foreign and Domestic"

I will oppose all those who are hostile to the provisions of this Nation, and who seek to change it by threat or action. This includes those who seek to impose their government or philosophy which is contrary to our Nation's beliefs. I realize that the individual, group or nations which threaten us could include American citizens or foreigners, or a combination of both.

"That I Will Bear True Faith and Allegiance to the Same"

In both word and deed, I will continue to express my devotion and loyalty to our constitution and government. I have an obligation to uphold it and will do nothing which could be interpreted as possessing a lack of confidence or belief in our nation.

"And That I Will Obey The Orders of the President of the United States"

The Commander in Chief holds ultimate authority to lead the United States Military as a means to protect our nation and our way of life. As outlined in our laws, the military serves the democratically elected leader of this nation.

"And the Orders of the Officers Appointed Over Me"

I acknowledge that officers are placed in positions of leadership over me and are responsible to maintain order and discipline in a military environment, while executing duties to accomplish assigned missions and tasks.

"According to Regulations and the Uniform Code of Military Justice"

As the military operates worldwide, and within unique circumstances, there is a special system of laws and courts to help maintain good order and discipline. This system protects my rights while a member of the military.

"So Help Me God"

With a belief in a Supreme Being, I make this covenant of conscience and invoke assistance of a higher power in fulfilling the obligations of this oath to society.

This oath is made of my own free will, and not under false pretenses.

Chapter 22

Essays and poems

LONG LIVE THE CONSTITUTIONAL Republic Declaration 2021

When in the course of American events, it becomes necessary for the citizenry to dissolve the political bands which have connected them with a despotic government, and to assume among the powers of the earth, the separate and equal station to which the laws of nature and of Nature's God entitle them, a decent respect to the opinions of mankind requires that they should declare the causes which impel them to the separation. We hold these truths to be self-evident, that all men are created equal, that they are endowed by their creator with certain unalienable rights, that among these rights are life, liberty, and the pursuit of happiness.

That to secure these rights, governments are instituted among men, deriving their just powers from the consent of the governed. That whenever any form of government becomes destructive of these ends, it is the right of the people to alter or to abolish it, and institute new government, laying its foundation on such principles and organizing its power in such form, as to them shall seem most likely to affect their safety and happiness. Prudence indeed will dictate that governments long established should not be changed for light and transient causes, and accordingly all experience has shown, that mankind are more disposed to suffer, while evils are sufferable, then to right themselves by abolishing the forms to which they are accustomed. But when a long train of abuses and usurpations, pursuing invariably the same object evinces a design to reduce them under absolute despotism, it is their right, it is their duty, to throw off such government, and to provide new guards for their future security. Such has been the patient sufferance of these colonies, and such is now the necessity which constrains them to alter their former systems of government. The history of this current version of tyranny, is a history of repeated injuries and usurpations, all having in direct the establishment of an absolute tyrannical grip over these states, to prove this, let facts be submitted to a candid world.

They (the federal government) have refused their assent to laws, the Constitution, the most wholesome and necessary to the public good.

They (the federal government) have superseded the sovereignty of the states, by inserting an authoritarian imperial jurisdiction contrary to the Constitution.

They (the federal government) have claimed a supremacy jurisdiction, out of the right and authority to fairly regulate.

They (the federal government) have illegally delegated law making powers out of the Congress, with the creation of the USC, putting that power in the hands of the executive branch administrative agencies.

They (the federal government) have sent our brothers, sisters, husbands, wives, sons, and daughters, to far off places to fight, die, kill, and be maimed for life in revenue generating wars that have nothing to do with defending our borders or liberty. And then failing to properly care for those Americans upon their return.

They (the federal government) have erected a multitude of new offices, and sent hither swarms of officers to harass our people, and eat out their substance.

They (the federal government) have made judges dependent on their will alone, for the tenure of their offices, and the amount and payment of their salaries.

They (the federal government) have kept among us, in times of peace, standing armies contrary to the Constitution.

They (the federal government) have affected to render the military independent of and superior to the civil power.

They (the federal government) have combined the three separate branches of government, to subject us to a jurisdiction foreign to our Constitution, and unacknowledged by our laws, giving their assent to their pretended acts of legislation:

For quartering large bodies of troops among us.

For protecting them from punishment for any murders they should commit on the inhabitants of these states.

For imposing taxes without our consent.

For depriving us in many cases of a trial by jury, and terrorizing us into plea agreements that go against the right to not incriminate yourself.

They (the federal government) have constrained our fellow citizens to bear arms against their country, to become the executioners of their friends and brethren, or to fall themselves by their hand in order to survive.

In every stage of these oppressions we have petitioned for redress in the most humble terms. Our petitions have been answered only by repeated injury. We have appealed to our native justice and Constitutionality, and we have conjured them by the ties of our common kindred to disavow these usurpations, which, would inevitably interrupt our connections and correspondence. They too have been deaf to the voice of justice and of consanguinity. We must therefore, acquiesce in the necessity, which denounces our separation, and hold them, as we hold the rest of mankind, enemies in war, in peace friends.

We, therefore, representatives of The Sovereign United States of America, in general congress, assembled, appealing to the Supreme judge of the world for the rectitude of our intentions, do, in the name, and by the authority of the good people of these free states, solemnly publish and declare, that these United States are, and of right ought to be free and independent states. That they are absolved from all allegiance to the never intended federal empire, and that all political connections between them and the tyrannical federal entity, is and ought to be totally dissolved, and that as free and independent states, they have full power to levy war, conclude peace, contract alliances, establish commerce, and to do all other acts and things which independent states may of right do. And for the support of this declaration, with a firm reliance on the protection of divine providence, we mutually pledge to each other our lives, our fortunes, and our sacred honor!

The Absence of True Scales of Justice, Allowed Weaponization

While all eyes are focused on the executive branch administrative agency, the Department of Justice, and rightly so, corruption and criminality are a common procedure. This is not new. There's evidence that dates back to the '60s of FBI murders, and attempted staged crimes. Men accused of killing Malcolm X released, now that the planted "informants / CHS's" are dead and can't testify to the truth. The murder of the Black Panther, Hugh Newton, is the movie that showcases "Judas and the Black Messiah." The list of murdered Americans, and staged crimes by the FBI, has increased exponentially ever since, with no accountability! The phrase of today's partisans is: "no one is above the law." Since when? I'll answer that question. It's been ever since the judicial branch abandoned the unbiased scales of justice, for "viewing the evidence in the light most favorable to the government!" Federal judges have a career appointment with no oversight. The only condition to their office is " in good behavior," with no one to judge a judge for good behavior! Most judges are appointed to the office having first been prosecutors for the government, or AUSA's. So having spent much of their time as such, their natural inclination is more open to the arguments of the prosecution. When you couple that with the beliefs of political parties, who have zero regard for the inalienable rights of citizens, as provided by the supreme law of the land, the Constitution, it's apparent why the "justice" system has become so askew in its precedence! There is no interest in justice, or the truth of the matter! Only a favorable outcome for the government. If that means covering up criminal practices by law enforcement, or the prosecution, so be it. If the government wins, the courts win, right? Until both lose the confidence of the people they govern! Courts seemed to be interested in protecting the integrity of their own institutions before the Civil War. Even in 1932, Justice Roberts cited the importance of maintaining that integrity. As the government has become more aggressive, the courts have left justice in a heap, for conviction by any means! Instead of being the pillar that weighs justice on the scale, courts are bias at the onset of a case. This condition in your "justice" system, corruption and criminality in your law enforcement is allowed to run rampant! The land of the free, home of the brave, has an alarming population of innocent citizens incarcerated! How does a population maintain faith in such a system?

It's Only Democracy to Provide Fall Guys for the Bureaucracy
    Did you ever wonder how the director of the FBI could go before Congress and refuse to answer their questions? Or how an FBI agent can appear before Congress and mock them

with silly and inappropriate faces? Do you scratch your head wondering who the president is referring to when he says he's going to get in trouble for saying too much, as he's leaving the podium? These questions thrusted me into a study of how the Constitutional Republic was transformed. Our country was formed with a document that dictated what the federal government could do. It was a contract between the people, and the government, which delegated powers to the federal entity, and constrained its ability to usurp the sovereignty of the states. That document, the Constitution, is the supreme law of the United States of America. It's sworn upon by every official who seeks public office, as well as every soldier called on to defend our nation and our liberty.

Our government has abandoned this legally binding contract. It has developed its own set of rules which is known as the United States Code or the USC. The USC dictates how the government operates entirely. What was once known as Article 1 of the Constitution, which grants the legislative branch of the government its powers and duties, now exists as Title 2 of the USC. Article 2 of The Constitution which creates the executive branch, and outlines the president's duties, is now title 3 of the USC. In title 3, section 301, the powers of the president are secretly delegated to "the head of any department or agency in the executive branch." This means that any department head, any agency head in the executive branch, is "empowered" with the same authority as the president, without having been elected or approved by the American people. countless unknown people, with no accountability, dictating changes in America.

How can Congress, who are supposed to write the acts of Congress, the laws, stand before news reporters and say that "they were asked to vote on a bill that they didn't have time to read?" Their job was to write the bills, not read them! It is because Title 2, sections 4101 and 4301, allow them to appoint officers to do their jobs for them, and committees of elected, unelected, and lobbyists to make laws governing Americans.

This explains how big business manipulates laws to maximize profits, while deteriorating the quality of American lives. Where has article 3 of the Constitution, or the Judicial branch of government been throughout these breaches of our Constitution? In the 2020 edition of the USC, they were found in Title 28 which changed in 2021. Speaking of changes, the last appearance of our founding documents was in the 2010 edition of the USC under "Organic Laws," which didn't even merit a designation with a "title." Sadly having been appointed by Republicans and, by their adversaries, Democrats, and without regard to the previous studies of history found in court proceedings by actual justices, they have become dependent on their tyrannical parties for the tenure of their offices, and the amount and payment of their salaries, which is straight out of the Declaration of Independence. In 1863, CJ Lowry of the Pennsylvania Supreme Court, citation [45 PA. 238, 1863 WL 4874 (PA. 1863)], wrote, "Our jealousy of the usurpation of dominant parties is quite natural," citing the experiences of both Britain and the early colonies. He went on to say, "Our fathers saw these dangers, and intended the Constitution to stand as a restraint upon party power." And also, "They knew how Episcopalians, Independants, and Presbyterians, Cavalier and Roundhead, Court and Country, Whig and Tory parties, had each, in turn, when in power, tyrannized over their opponents, and sacrificed or endangered public liberty." The courts of today ignore such knowledge and insight, opting for the prior findings of flawed recent cases, known as case law, which all but ignores the Constitutional rights of individuals in order to bury the United States taxpayer in a never-ending perpetual debt.

What initiated the sequence of events that seemingly obliterated the Constitution? Oddly enough, in my studies, it looks like "Reorganization Plans" which first appear in 1939, and were invoked by the president. These plans pull power to the executive branch, consolidating all three branches into executive branch administrative agencies that run America.

Imagine the one person whose sole duty is to defend the Constitution, being the one to trample it to the furthest degree! And the Supreme court, which in 1803 ruled "that an act of Congress repugnant to the Constitution cannot become a law," and in the same case Marbury v. Madison 5 U.S. 137, Cranch 137, 2 L. ED. 60, ruled "the president cannot authorize a secretary of state to omit the performance of those duties which are enjoined by law." So how was a president allowed to do just that? Why wasn't it stopped by the legislative or judicial branch? That was already answered. "For the tenure of their offices, and the amount and payment of their salaries." America has been sold out by the very people who have been chosen to oversee the public good. There's no dismissing real facts as "conspiracy theories" when the facts are proven true! No "official" office has protected the individual Constitutional rights of citizens nor the public good!

Standing Army Isn't Militia

In the United States Constitution, you'll find two terms pertaining to defense. The first is the "standing army," which is made up of paid, trained, professional soldiers. Our founding fathers dealt with Britain's standing army, as well as other standing armies that were rented to fight against the colonies. The force of mercenaries (rented standing army), was known as the "Hessians." Britain's standing army, before the revolution, was as we find ourselves in the last 70 years, a deployed peacekeeping / police force. Their duty was to maintain the peace and domestic tranquility. As King George III dealt more harshly with the colonies and taxes, and ability to participate in trade and commerce, naturally the rise of hostility manifested itself. Before it came to shots being fired, there were acts of mischief, throwing of rocks and snowballs, and damage to incoming British freight. But a standing army only knows one thing, overwhelm the opposition with superior tactics and violence in order to achieve victory. Standing armies only know one thing, escalate to a superior violence, win. This is the main reason why Americans should be alarmed by the militarization of our police. The Constitution only allowed for standing armies to be funded for two years at a time, and only as needed for defense. Today we have five branches of full-time military, millions of armed federal agents, and now police are becoming standing armies. Our nation's framers knew that paid professional soldiers (standing army), are subordinate to whoever signs their paycheck! It's a very beautiful thought to believe that the civil body politic in power, will utilize their just powers for good. That they will exhibit good behavior, and reframe themselves from corruption. The founding fathers studied the demise of history's republics, and sought not to repeat them by limiting the federal authority in order to prevent tyranny. And if those contractual/Constitutional limitations should be usurped and violated, they built a safeguard. "Well regulated militia being necessary for the security of a free state!" The militia is made up of citizens who have families and strong ties to their communities. They are moral, rational people, who are human beings first. Warfare and violence do not feed their families. Militia was intended to be the conscience, and last line of defense for the land of the free and home of the brave. Congress neglected their duty to see the maintenance of the militia, to expand the "World Police Force," which is what our military has become. The federal law enforcement community has sought to instigate and frame crimes in order to create fear of the militia! Has the federal government become the enemy of a free state? And why be afraid of people who would serve in your defense at their own expense? Free of charge, at a time when inflation and debt are ruining our country. I trust my neighbors more than paycheck chasers! Paid soldiers are mercs, militia are citizens who train for your defense on their own time and expense. Bring the conscience back to those

who volunteer to defend! Support your local militia! God bless
and long live the Constitutional Republic!

What Are We Dying For?

You say that I'm dangerous, because my stance is set;

There's things you don't like to remember, and I can't soon
forget.

Men crossing a river in the winter, many not wearing shoes;

Fear in all their hearts, but freedom is too much to lose.

Bound together by a common goal, bled together to be
achieved;

But our unity would be tried, and three quarters of a million
to be grieved.

We'd get pulled into World War One, which I don't think was
our fight;

I guess between killing each other and natives, we lost track
of what is right.

We would soon bleed again in Europe, leaving lots of Americans dead;

Our blood soaked the beaches of Normandy, and stained the
water red.

Next we die in Korea, defending the south from the north;

Not defending our borders, but our army would still go forth.

Onto the jungles of Vietnam, we found a slaughterhouse
there;

Fighting the spread of communism, now it's here no one
seems to care.

Then we declared against terror, which took us to
Afghanistan and Iraq;

Fighting an inanimate object, in a narrative unsupported by
fact.

Our lives are being spent, not in defense or remaining free;

Which might make sense to you, but it's not logical to me.

Now they say we're our biggest threats, the enemy is patriots within;

When will you question what they say, how many Americans will it cost to win?

A Republic If You Can Keep It

We no longer have that Republic. It didn't disintegrate into a democracy, nor a monarchy, but a bureaucratic dictatorship. How could such a solid Republic slip from the grip of American citizens? Were we so easily duped, that we handed our rights over to the first person to ask for them? Were we so gullible to believe that executive branch administrative agencies, some run by "health professionals," can decide what's best for the body, rather than the one who lives in it? Or do we ask a bigger question: was the republic built to be kept? As soon as Earth was created and man occupied it, a plot to sabotage perfection was being set in place. Why would we think anything less for our own Republic? In 1803, Marbury v. Madison took the court by storm with fighting a president exercising unlawful authority. 16 years after our sacred document, the Constitution was ratified, the question of the authority of the executive branch acting in derogation of the Constitution was posed. Why would legislators want to make laws opposed to the Constitution, if they lived during the same time as the Constitution was written? They saw the document put in effect, some watched it set in place, and yet citizens were okay with derogating from the very document that built their home? Even Jefferson, being a founding father, was drunk with power. This is why the checks and balances exist, but the courts are not enforcing the supreme law of the land. They are "construing" more authority to the federal government than is afforded in the Constitution. The court in 1803, being untainted by partisan politics, was more willing to do its job, as compared to present day partisans, granting more power than intended for the parties to rule with an iron fist. Thousands of unconstitutional statutes later and hundreds of agencies with unconstitutionally delegated powers, and we wonder why our "American dream is so tasteless?" No, we do not have a Republic if you can keep it, but a bureaucratic dictatorship if you can dismantle it.

Take Our Guns, Stop the Killing

Those who lack logic, want to steal your Constitutional right.

Because of their own lack of courage, they'd inhibit your ability to fight.

Perhaps they don't recall, or maybe they choose not to remember.

A day America lost over 3,000 lives, the saddest day 11 September.

No firearms were brandished, not a shot fired in anger.

Box cutters were the tool, no law can prevent danger.

In Chicago, murder is illegal and seemingly the killing never stops.

Despite the firmest gun control, or its multitude of cops.

We claim to be a society progressing, but our actions say that we're insane.

The more we restrict the second amendment, the more ground evil seems to gain.

Why not scare bad people, by using a lesson from the past?

When they seek a victim, finding a rifle behind every blade of grass.

Strength deters aggression, as courage always wins the day.

After 91 years of restrictions, our thoughts have been one way.

Your government welcomes the slaughter, they enjoy decisions made out of fear.

While they publicly denounce the violence, tightening control power they hold dear.

Stop making yourselves victims, through panic and irrational thought.

Remember you have liberty, with American blood freedom was bought.

How Can We Be the United States and Have the FBI?

The Federal Bureau of Investigation was built to take on organized crime, originally. It didn't take long until they started targeting every form of organization. And peaceful, non-violent assemblies were no exception. Dr. Martin Luther King Jr. was victimized by the FBI, simply for wanting the very equality that America is supposed to stand for. In fact, since then and now, concerned parents have become targets of the FBI, simply for being concerned over the sexual indoctrination their children are receiving in public schools. Every form of peaceful unification among Americans, ends up being infiltrated by the FBI, and led to, and coerced to participate in crime. This has been the case since the sixties! It's now 2023, over 80 years of intentional sabotage of unity, and by an agency that calls itself "law enforcement." How does this go on for over 80 years before a "Weaponization Committee" gets formed? The crimes that have been orchestrated against the people, by the FBI, have long been discovered! Murders, agency planned conspiracies, extortions, taking over criminal enterprises, blackmail, and deprivation of rights, I could go on, but my point is made! The Federal Bureau of Investigation has become the very thing that it was built to take on. Instead of the highest law enforcement agency of the land, it has evolved into the most powerful organized crime syndicate on the planet! Complete with courts that support and cover up the criminal activity. It can be truly said, "United we stand, divided we fall!" How can we stand united with our own government attacking our unity? Who will stand up to criminals who carry government badges? Does anyone else care about the survival of the United States of America? The damage to our country is at epic proportions! We have never been more divided. Add to it the unavoidable economic strain of reckless spending, which will put financial strain on every middle and lower class household. There comes a point in a nose dive, where catastrophe is unavoidable. Forgive me for feeling as though we are near that point. If we are to right this ship, it will only be through unity! And real history reflects that this country isn't big enough for both unity and the FBI to exist within its borders. May Americans realize and accept the truth, have the courage to write the wrongs, and God bless and long live the Constitutional Republic!

Untitled

It is my opinion that Congress has a long-standing record of neglect in its powers and duties in regard to the militia. This dereliction has, in my mind, not been unintentional. The lack of personal responsibility on the part of men in society has led to a decline, which in turn, has been used to weaponize fear and sacrifice liberty in the name of supposed public good. Charging the taxpayer currency for an ineffective fix, illegally delegating its law making authority, failing to represent the voice of those who have elected them, and transforming the "land of the free and home of the brave," into the over-policed and supremely terrorized American people. This neglect has not gone unnoticed, in fact it has provoked another form of despotism from the executive branch. Completely ignoring the doctrine of the separation of powers, the executive branch has swollen to not only accommodate Congress' duty, "to call forth the militia to execute the laws of the Union," but also to adopt unconstitutional standing armies to both write laws in the form of policy making and "enforcing" its own rules without any proper jurisdiction, and complete disregard for the sovereignty of the states and the union of the Republic. And how has the judicial branch responded to these trespasses upon the Constitution, the supreme law of our land? They have sacrificed their integrity, and the dignity of their office, in order to trade American freedom away, putting liberty and inalienable rights on the auction block of partisan politics. Justices have ruled on the dangers of two major party systems, and given multitudes of insight on how treacherous these two opposing forces can be to a free society. Instead of heeding those warnings, judges have plummeted to the very depths of being, "dependent on," the will of their political party, "for the tenure of their offices, and the amount and payment of their salaries." In fact, all three branches of our Constitutionally constructed government should go back and read the Declaration of Independence, in order to understand the reasons which impelled our separation from the British. They would see that our plight in this day far exceeds 1776. Which brings us back to the subject of purposefully degenerating American men from an interior position, treasonously reducing our society with dramatic effect.

How The Constitutional Republic Is Broken

Title 5, Part 1, Chapter 8, Section 801-808, outlines how agencies make our laws, not Congress, as our Constitution dictates. These agencies also dictate federal budget spending and allocations to illegal government "independent" companies. Covid-19 was back door funded exactly in this fashion, and over 3 million people died, with no accountability. There is no legal, federal jurisdiction for these agencies. The federal government is not allowed to supersede state jurisdiction. Anything that deviates from the Constitution, may not operate. (Marbury v. Madison and Bayard v. Singleton)

About the Authors

Theresa Nichols

I am a Christian Constitutionalist who was seeking The River of God in the midst of a Demonic Tsunami that had hit America in 2020. My search began in late 2019 when God's Spirit warned me of an impending devastation coming to America.

My search for The River took me into the demonic depth of the occult that is deeply embedded and driving the direction of our broken republic. God sent a man who had The River of God gushing out of him and into my life. The man is the hero of this book and has become the son of my very heart and soul.

Tessie Liz Nichols soon to be Croft

I am a Christian Constitutionalist who was seeking for the how and why this bureaucracy killed our republic. My fiance, the love of my life, my hero, my Gunboat, gave me truth, light, logic, and answers.

The United States Code is a defacto document that controls this country. Delegation of authority and administrative promulgation has run our republic into the ground. Barry Gordon Croft Jr. defines me. I am bone of his bone and flesh of his flesh, his Constitutional soulmate for eternity and in all dimensions.

www.ingramcontent.com/pod-product-compliance
Lightning Source LLC
Chambersburg PA
CBHW070027030426
42335CB00017B/2325